KINDLE
FIRE HD

MANUAL

FOR **NEWCOMERS**

How to use Fire HD tablet like a pro:
guide to managing kindle library and
content

Stephen W. Rock

Dedicated to all my readers

Acknowledgement

Ii want to say a very big thank you to Michael Lime, a 3D builder, my colleague. He gave me moral support throughout the process of writing this book.

Table of Contents

Introduction

This is a very easy guide for new users of the Kindle Fire HD 8 and 10 devices. Written with precision and simplicity, this guide offers valid advice for optimizing the Kindle device you just got.

This first part of this guide is an introduction into what a Kindle device is. The second part delves into matters relating to managing kindle books, sharing kindle books, downloading stuffs on your Fire tablet, and troubleshooting a Kindle Fire device. The last part of the book covers tips and tricks for optimizing your kindle device.

Haven highlighted issues that are most prevailing to new kindle device owners/users in this book, you can be rest assured of value for money.

Now, it's time get started. Enjoy your read.

Chapter 1

Getting Started With Your Kindle Device

A kindle is a device like a tablet that is used for reading books. The creation of these devices was started in 2007 by Amazon. You know how you use a MP3 player for downloading music, so it is with the Kindle for books. You can download books wirelessly and read at you own convenience.

The kindle fire was released in 2012 and it is said to have perform more than the kindle devices before it. It uses Android Operating System and can be said to be similar to a tablet. But you have more freedom with this device. Together with being able to read books, you can even stream music and also video.

How reading works is that users of the kindle device download Kindle editions from the website of Amazon. Kindle editions are e-books that have been made for viewing on the Kindle device. Users actually prefer to use Wi-Fi connections to download but newer versions of the kindle enable 3G phone technology. With this you have the ability to access and download the books anywhere you may be.

In fact if you would prefer, you can download them on your PC and them move them to your device. You can use a USB cable for this.

Something users love about this device is that unlike the ancient times when you read from hard copy, moving the books around can be uncomfortable. For those who love to read when going on vacations, they have to load their luggages with dozens of books and carrying it around is a big deal.

But with the Kindle, oh, it's an answer to problems. You can download a massive number of books and that doesn't mean it will get any heavier. Why would it, it's a device. It is very convenient and handy. With a 6-inch screen, reading is a delight. The little keyboard helps to search the web and other operations that require typing.

Chapter 2

How To Set Up And Manage Your Kindle Device

Okay you've just gotten your Kindle. You're happy, I can see. Time to get your reading game on. But wait you haven't used this kind of device before and you have no idea how to run it. How then would you start things and enjoy your e-reader. No need to panic. Read to the end and see how to get the best of your Kindle.

Set up Wi-Fi

First things first, connect to a Wi-Fi. When you purchased your kindle, you'll be asked to connect t a Wi-Fi network as you're setting it up. Maybe you didn't have a wireless network available at the moment so you hit **Set Up Wi-Fi Later**. Yu access Wi-Fi after your initial setup

1. Enter the **Menu**
2. Go to **Settings**
3. Select **Wi-Fi Networks.**
4. The device should start to scan for wireless networks that are near you.
5. Select the your network and put in the password (if you set a password)

If you're not near your network, you can even try to set up with a public hotspot. But you will still add your own network once your home. If your Kindle allow as for 3G mobile connection, you can use that without much ado and avoid the step for Wi-Fi. Though it will still be good if you add a Wi-Fi network as this is usually faster.

Register

Registering your kindle is the next thing to do. When you're first setting up your kindle, you have the option to either register with an existing account or create a new one. When you select our preferred choice, follow the direction it pastes on screen.

If you've already registered and have bought a Kindle book or books, you can start stacking them by using the home page section for Cloud. You device comes with a user's manual already and also dictionaries, but just like everyone you probably want something more thrilling. If you're using one of the previous kindle versions, setting up might take a bit more time as you can't tap the letters but use the directional pad to navigate.

But it doesn't matter, you won't much type in. After you've registered and set Wi-Fi up, all you'll be doing is the thing you bought the Kindle for; reading

And yeah, it will ask you to enter your account on Goodreads. Also a Twitter and Facebook account. But you can always turn to the bottom of the display for the skip button. After this, it will make you go through a tutorial. Go through it as you'll find how to summon the toolbar, turn pages, enter dictionary, alter the backlight and other cool features.

Now your Kindle will want have some knowledge about the kind of books you prefer. It will ask you to choose your preferred genres and rate about

10 books. You will then be asked to sign up for Kindle Unlimited and it may even give you some book samples to download for free.

Getting the books

People love Amazon because buying books on the website in any genres so easy. But one thing they also love is that they can spend a lot of time reading   classics that are free. This is because Amazon made it so that you can get any book made before 1923. Any book that was published prior to 1923, is out of copyright and is in the domain of the public so it's out of copyright

Do you know what that means. It's a book fiesta. You can get well over 2 million selections. To begin with this, make sure you get hold of as many titles as you can from Amazon. But since your Kindle does not do ePub files, you can go to Internet Archive, look through, select a title and choose Kindle so that you can download it on your computer.

Now connect your PC to your Kindle with a USB cable. Move the file or files you've just downloaded to your Kindles folder. If you're using a Kindle that works with 3G networks you can get it with email directly.

1. Enter the **Menu**
2. Go to **Settings**
3. Then **Device Options**
4. If you move to the bottom of the screen you should find the email address of your Kindle.

Get even more books

This feature is kind of new to Amazon. It's the ability to borrow books. Yeah I said borrow books. One way is through public libraries using Overdrive. This differs depending on your location so you want to be sure to check the website of your library so that you can see how they work and if they work with Kindle.

For those who are members of Amazon Prime there's another way to so it. Amazon Prime costs $99 for every year and gives you nice benefits like free two-day shipping on the things sold by Amazon. You do the borrowing through **Amazon Kindle Lending Library.** With this you are able to borrow 1 book a month. You'll be able to get access to titles on the list if the New York Times bestseller.

To get to the Lending Library,
1. Enter the **Kindle Store** on your tablet
2. Choose the dropdown for the menu called **All Categories**
3. Move all the way down to the bottom of the listed options

There's a new function that are available to Prime members. Limitless access to a rotating tiles collection. Another one for the Prime members is the **Kindle Unlimited.** You subscribe to it and you have limitless access to a selection of comics and magazines.

Fine-tune Fonts

You might not know the name of the fonts you like but that doesn't mean you still don't have your preferred choice when it comes to fonts. Maybe you saw a font style on a Newspaper and it just caught your eye.

And you can make the fonts on your Kindle dance to your tune. You have the ability to adjust the fonts as you read the book (now you don't get that with hard copy books). To be able to use this feature

1. Hit the top part of your display.
2. Select the option for **Aa**
3. From you can select your font style and size

You have the possibility of choosing up to 8 sizes for the texts. And you have 9 different font selections.

You also have the option to choose font spacing. This will make you be able to select 3 line spacing options and also the margin size. If you're using the Kindle Oasis, you have the opportunity to adjust the orientation to you taste, you can read in portrait mode if you like

Block the kindle from your account

If it so happens that you lose you kindle device or if it was stolen, you want to detach the device from your account immediately. Like A.s.a.p. You should do so because the person who stole it will definitely want to check out your contents and read for free the books you've bought with your own earned money.

What's even worse is that if the thief knows how to handle the device, he can even purchase more books on the Kindle with your credit card info.

So you want to make sure you deregister the Kindle from your account as quick as you can. Grab a PC and

1. Enter a Web Browser
2. Sign in to your account on Amazon
3. Select Your Account
4. Go to **Manage Your Content and Devices**.
5. Choose **Your Devices**
6. Select the device you want to deregister
7. Look for **Deregister**

Put Kindle Apps on your other devices

One thing we love about the kindle is the ability to install its apps on a wide range of devices. You have the option to install on Windows phones, Android, iOS, Mac or PC.

When you install the Kindle apps on the devices you have that are compatible, you have the ability to sync what you read currently and your subscriptions with them. This doesn't not replace your Kindle. Your kindle is armed a lasting battery, E-link display and a nice portable design.

But when you do this you can continue your reading anywhere anytime. You know those messed up times when you forget to take you Kindle with you? at least you can continue your reading with the device that you're with at the moment.

Control Access

You have the ability of setting parental controls by restricting the access on your Kindle to the Web browser, Goodreads or The Kindle store.

1. Go to **Menu**
2. Choose **Settings**
3. Select **Parental Controls**
4. Then **Restrictions**

With this you can start Kindle FreeTime. This makes it possible for you to make a tailored profile for your child and you'll be able to put in suitable contents.

To do the Family Access
1. Tap **Menu**
2. Select **Household and family library**
3. Then **Add a New Person**

From here you can make a Household of 2 grownups and manage child accounts of up to 4. If you want to, you can even create a Family Library. This allows you to share with devices or Kindle apps books or contents.

Chapter 3

How to transfer content to your Kindle Fire

Transferring different contents to your Kindle Fire using its micro-USB connector is quite easy. You can transfer music, videos, photos, and documents. However, personal content transferred to your Kindle Fire HD 8 or 10 is stored only on your device and will not be found in cloud.

To successfully transfer contents from your computer to your Kindle Fire HD, take the following steps:

1. Connect Kindle Fire t your computer with a micro-USB cable. The cable is sold separately.
2. Slide the arrow from right to left to unlock your Kindle Fire.
3. Launch pen your Kindle Fire drive on your computer

4. Drag and drop your content in the applicable content folder you want. I.e. music or video.

5. When you are done referring content, tap the Disconnect button at the bottom of your Kindle Fire HD screen and eject it from your computer. Unplug the cable.

Chapter 4

How To Delete Books From Your Kindle Library

So you've bought your Kindle for some time now. You've downloaded, you've read, rinse repeat. You've amassed so many books of different kinds. And now your library is packed with content. Kindles are wonderful devices but no matter how much space it has, it will get full someday.

And maybe today is that day. So why don't we get rid of some titles now. We'll go through how to remove books from your device so that you can finally put in brand new stuffs. And we all are excited when we get a new book to read.

Let's get this started. First you should know that since you've purchased the book, you have the right to read the book. So if you remove it, it's still in the cloud so you can download it again if you want it back. But since you've removed it, it does no longer take up space.

1. Go to the book you want to banish. You can find it in the library. If you cannot find it, you can always use the search and input the keyword of the book

2. After you've found the book you've been looking for, Tap and hold it for a while and a list of options should show up on the display. This method only works for the Kindles that are equipped with touchscreen. If your Kindle is the one with the directional controls, hit the left directional key instead as the title is selected so that you can summon the list of options.

3. Scan through the list for **Remove from Device**. You might not see that exact name. It depends on the version of your kindle. But you find something similar to that. Select that option.

If happens that you long pressed and tapped **Remove from device** accidentally, you can always connect wirelessly to download it again. Just make sure you have an internet connection and put in you login details.

Chapter 5

Step By Step Guide To Delete A Book From The Kindle Library

When it comes to deleting books from your kindle, it all comes down to your choice. There are about 3 methods to do this. All offer different perks and disadvantages. In this detailed guide, we'll learn the ways of how you can delete a book from your device. Depending on the method you prefer, you can start to remove and flush away those unwanted items.

Ways To Delete A Book From Your Kindle Fire Tablet

1. Long pressing and clicking the **Remove from device** option

2. Going through with your PC and entering **Manage Your Content and Devices** section to remove completely.

3. Deregistering your device

First Method

With this method, you will be able to clear the book from your device. All the record of you purchases will still be stored. All that happens is that the book is no longer in your kindle so your space is freed in a way.

Step 1
Enter the home screen. To go to the home screen on your kindle, you have to press the black and white symbol of a house. When you enter the home screen, you'll be able to access the Kindle library so as to reveal the books

Step 2
Track down the book you want to delete. You want scroll down to find the book but if you've searched and you can't find the title, you can hit the magnifying glass at the top right corner of

the screen. From here, type in the title of the book or you can put a key word on the search field

Step 3
When the book has been discovered, Tap and hold the title of the book. When you do that, you'll be given a menu of options. From the provided list of options, select the one that says **Remove From Device**. Once you tap this option, the book will be deleted from your kindle.

Second Method

Okay, now you may want more. The first method only gives you the opportunity to remove the book from the Kindle. But other information of the book and of you buying the book are still stored. So for those trying to cover their tracks so that people don't actually find out that you bought a particular book, this one's for you. Operation Clean sweep

Step 1

Get your computer and open up a web browser. Enter the amazon website and log in to your account to access your online content library. Enter **Manage Your Content and Devices**

Step 2

Now you want to be sure that the page you're in is **Your Content**. Once you've signed in to your account on amazon, the tab you'll be give may not be **Your Content**. So if the tab in front of you is another one, navigate and select **Your Content**

Step 3

Now you'll be given a list of the contents that are in your content library. Navigate and choose the book you desire to delete. Now at the far left of the display, you'll see a section of boxes named **Select**. With each row of books, you have a Select box. Mark the box beside the book you desire to remove.

Step 4

Navigate to the top left area of the page. You should see the **Delete** button right near the button for **Deliver**. You press this delete button and the item or items you've marked will be deleted

Step 5

But wait, it's not deleted yet, a menu will pop up to ask you confirm your obliteration of the item. You confirm that you want to delete and that it's not a mistake by selecting the **Yes, Delete Permanently** option. If it's a mistake and you accidentally marked and clicked the previous delete button, just don't click this option.

There's another security checkpoint asking you click **OK** to delete.

Third Method

If it so happens that you lose your Kindle, you can make it so that no one can access your books and contents by deregistering your device from your account. If you do this, you can be sure that none of your contents are left on the device. This will also be beneficial if you want to sell your Kindle.

But you should note that when you deregister this device, the items that are removed won't be accessible on this particular device unless you register it again.

Step 1

Grab your computer and head over to the amazon website. Log in to your account

Step 2

Head over to the **Manage Your Content and Devices** section. When you go over the button your account you should see the section.

Step 3

After that, move over the **Your Devices** tab. After clicking this option, you should see a list showing you all the devices you have linked to your account. Go to the device that you want to deregister and click. The device will become pink and the outline will be orange to signify that it has been selected.

Step 4

Look under the list of your the devices connected to your account for the **Deregister** button. After selecting the device, hit this button. Once you do this, the device will be detached from your account therefore all the books will be cleared form the Kindle.

Chapter 6

Sharing Kindle Books with Family and Friends

The Amazon's eBook reader has an ever-growing library. Amazon has made it possible for you to share its over six million books with your acquaintances. But this can be a little tricky. In a bid to help you do so easily, I have outlined in clear, detailed steps, how to share kindle books.

Family Library allows up to two adults and four children share their apps, single books, and audio books with one another. Regardless of whether they're using Kindle Paperwhite, Kindle Oasis, or any other an outdated Kindle Fire, members can read the same books at the same time without interrupting one another.

The first step to take in sharing kindle books with others is to grant them access to your Family Library. To do this, take the following steps:

1. Hit the **Manage Your Content and Devices** section of your Amazon account.
2. Below the **Settings** tab, in the **Households and Family Library** section, tap the **Invite an adult/invite a child** button.
3. The adult or child should enter their email and password in the spaces provided (or can create a new account if they have none).
4. Tap **Yes** to allow your account and that of the other share payment methods.
5. Select which book you'd like to share with the adult/child, and have them select which book they'd like to share with you.
6. Tap the **Finish** button.

Now that you have added adults and kids to your Family Library, you want to begin lending new kindle books. The following subheading highlights extensively how to do this.

1. Hit the **Manage Your Content and Devices** section of your Amazon account.
2. Select **the Show Family Library** link from the **Your Content** tab.
3. Select all the books you would like to share and click **Add to Library.**
4. Select a family member and click **OK.**

Downloading kindle books from your family library

Once you have received a kindle book from a family or friend, it's very easy to get it downloaded on your kindle e-reader. All you need to do is:

1. Hit the **Manage Your Content and Devices** section on your Amazon account.
2. Select the book(s) you'd like to send to your device or app, and click **Deliver**.
3. From the pop-up menu, select where the book(s) should go, and then click **Deliver** once more.

Sharing a kindle book from product page

Hitting a book's product page is quite an easy way to share kindle books. To get this done, simply do the following:

1. Hit the kindle store on your computer and type in the name of the book you want to loan.

2. Select the book from the resulting list.
3. On the product page, click **Loan this book**. You'd be directed to the **Loan this book** page where you can enter the recipients email address and an optional message.
4. Click **Send now**.

Downloading a loaned kindle book

You can also enjoy reading more books even if you do not have a Library card and new books aren't in your budget. You can request a book from a friend. Once the book is sent, you'd receive notifications on how to download it on your device. The following steps will help you.

1. Open the email message having the subject: **A Loaned Book for You**.
2. Click the **Get your loaned book now** button. This will open a link in your web browser.
3. Sign into your Amazon account and select the device you would like the book to be delivered to (in case you have a kindle e-book reader, Fire tablet, or kindle app).

4. Click the **Accept loaned book**.

5. If you don't have a Fire tablet, kindle e-book reader, or kindle app, you would need to follow the on-screen instructions to download the kindle app.

Note that you have only 14 days to read and return the book.

Chapter 7

Troubleshooting Your Kindle Fire

When we talk about android tablets, the line of the kindle fire tablets have been quite an accomplishment for Amazon. Ever since the fire tablet came into existence, it has been one upgrade after another. It even has the HD gives a wide range of content and comes in different sizes.

And we all know that when it comes to devices, most work well for our needs but even end the high end gadgets tend to have some hiccups and the Kindle fire is no exception.

However, not all encounter problems with their Kindle fire, the tablet is a wonderful device. But for the other set of people, here are some common problems affecting the fire that you may face and how to tackle them.

The fire just shows the logo

This is one problem that many face. The device doesn't start up correctly. It turns on quite all right but then it only makes it as far as the logo and it doesn't go anywhere else. Okay, you try to restart it, but then it will only take you to still the same logo. It's just gets frustrating a quite a lot of people have been looking for solution.

Solution

1. Plug the tablet to your computer and notice if the it will recognize our fire.
2. Try plugging your Kindle fire to the charger and do as you would charge normally. Let it sit there for a minimum of 15 minutes. Once the time is up, don't remove the charger. Still keep it plugged in and then long press the power button and wait for it to get past the logo checkpoint.
3. If you've tried and it doesn't work, it still shows the same problem, try communicating with Amazon Support.
4. Or we could go through it the hard way. Let's try and reach to the recovery menu. Put off the tablet then to put it back on,

long press the **Power** button and **Volume down** button at the same time. If your device does not turn on, try using the **Volume up** button. When it finally comes on and you're in the recovery menu, navigate through the options using the **Volume keys** and select with the **Power key**. With this you'll be able to do a factory reset. When you do this, it will clear everything on your device. (That's why you should always back up)

Kindle Fire Shows an internal error

When some use their tablet and they try to get into some apps, it gives a message saying **An internal error has occurred.** If your device starts behaving this way, do these

Solution

1. Try restarting your Fire. Press and hold the power key for about 20 seconds and then put it on.
2. Verify that the Time and Date of you tablet is accurate. To do this
    -   Slide downwards from the top of the display
    -   Choose **More**
    -   Then **Date & Time**
3. To remove any issues that have to do with connectivity, put off your internet router. After a few seconds, you can turn it back on.
4. Try to stop the app from working in the meantime
    -   Swipe downwards from the top
    -   Select **More**
    -   Then **Applications**
    -   Choose **Install applications**

5. Try deregistering you device by entering
   - **More**
   - Then **My account**
   - Select **Deregister**

   After deregistering, you can register again and check if there's any improvement.

Kindle fire won't charge

When using the kindle fire, some encounter issues with charging, it might charge rather slowly and for others it won't just charge

Solutions
1. To check if it's the fault of the device or the cable, try using the cable with another device ad see if will charge
2. Try putting you kindle fire off and plug in the charger
3. Be sure you're using the charger that came with your Kindle fire
4. When you're certain that the device has a problem and the light indicator does not turn on to show its charging, try fixing the cable a little bit more deep into the port.
5. If nothing works, you might have to contact Amazon

No audio from the fire

In the course of using your device, it might start to not give you audio.

Solution

1. Maybe it doesn't require anything techy, just put on your volume. To ensure that your volume is increased, press the **Volume Up** button.
2. Verify that nothing is plugged to the headphone jack of your tablet. If anything is plugged, there will be no external audio
3. Use a cover that's designed for the Kindle fire. Some covers are not meant to be used with the Fire. If you use them that may the reason you don't get audio.
4. Restart your device. To restart automatically, long press the power key for 40 seconds. If does not restart, turn you Kindle fire on normally.

The keyboard is misbehaving

Sometimes you might type something reasonable like **I will catch up with you soon** and on its own, the keyboard will to give out some random letters that's sometimes can be found on any dictionary on earth.

Solution

1. First off, maybe the keyboards perfectly fine. It might be it's the screen that's cluttered up with dust and oil from everyday hustle and bustle. Use a microfiber cloth to lean the screen. And make sure that there are no air bubbles under the screen protector
2. Try restating your Kindle fire.
3. Try factory resetting.
   - Go to **Settings**
   - Tap **Device**
   - Then **Reset to Factory Default**
   - Select **Reset**
   This will erase **everything** on the device. You know as the wise old men would rightly say, make sure to back up your device.
4. If issue still persists, go contact Amazon

Kindle Fire won't connect to computer

If you're trying to transfer files between your PC and Fire, sometimes it might just show that it has been disconnected or that it is no longer responding. Even worse, the device might not even show up at all.

Solution

1. Restart both your PC and tablet. Once the two devices turn back on, there's a chance that they might recognize themselves
2. It might be the cable you're using that has a problem. Try using another cable.
3. Don't rely solely on cables for transfer, try doing it wirelessly. You can do it through email. Dropbox is also there

Kindle Fire doesn't connect to Wi-Fi

Whatever makes your Kindle fire not to connect to a Wi-Fi network, try these solutions

Solution
1. Crosscheck that Airplane mode is not turned on. You might be sure that you don't remember putting it on but still crosscheck, maybe you did it by accident
2. Try putting your Kindle fire off and on. When it comes on, try connecting to a network again and see what happens
3. You might just have to reset to factory settings

Stubborn enough for the browser not to work

It's been well reported that the Silk browser, pre-installed on the devices gives users issues. It may crash continuously or just work very slowly.

Solution
1. Restart you Kindle fire by pressing the power key for 20 seconds and putting it on
2. Wipe all the data on the Silk
   - GO to **Settings**
   - Choose **Applications**
   - Then **Manage All Applications**
   - Select **Silk browser**
   - Hit **Clear Data**
3. Still not working? Forget about silk and use another browser. Word on the street is that Dolphin browser works as a nice replacement.

Chapter 8

Kindle Tips and Tricks

We are gradually coming to the end of this book. We will round off with tips and tricks for Kindle Fire 8 and 10 tablets.

Get free books

Now who hates free stuff? Let me see your hands up. Everyone likes to get things for free and you can do just that with your Amazon Kindle device. Be prepared to read classics though, because that's what's in store for you.

Now you really have no excuse for not reading Mark Twain because now you have the opportunity of downloading books for free. Yup, your balance remains untouched. Search the Amazon website and you'll find thousands of books for free. In fact not only Amazon, even with open library, you get the same offer.

Save for reading offline

With your kindle, reading online is really no biggie. You got the Silk so internet is no hassle. But the one you've probably never used much is the Instapaper. This works on virtually all device. Mac, iOS, Android, PC.

When you've selected your Kindle as the device you want to use to view offline in settings, all you do next time you want to save something to view offline is bookmark it and it be available in your account on Kindle. It will also be available to any devices that are connected to your account.

Reduce glare and fingerprints

One problem I have about the Kindle Fire tablet is its high amount of screen glare. I know many uses who don't like this too. Haven gone through feedbacks, I concluded that this might be a good place to start from. Well, this can be fixed. Simply apply a glare-reducing screen protector. They are available on Amazon.

Add more storage

The more you download movies on your Kindle Fire HD 10 tablet, the faster you are going to be running out of storage. So, get an extra storage. Samsung's 64GB microSD car sells at $20 .Good enough, it comes with an SD adapter in case you want to copy media for your adapter. If you do not feel comfortable getting an SD card for that amount, you can opt for other cheaper ones on Amazon. I use a microSD card of about 256 GB on my Fire tablet.

Watch movies copied from your computer

You do like the idea of having to buy every movie on the Amazon store. You can copy movies from your computer into your Kindle Fire tablet. To access these movies on your device, consider the following:

1. Go to Video>Library and open the hamburger menu.
2. Scroll to Personal Videos and tap. All your personal media will be found here.

Note that you cannot play AVI videos.

Manage notifications

You can control those disturbing notifications you don't want. If you find a particular app or game always sending you unwarranted notifications, then turn them off. To turn off notifications, simply follow the below steps:

1. Go to Settings > Sound and Notification > App Notifications
2. Tap on the app you want and block notifications.

Back up photos and videos

You can back up photos and videos to Amazon Drive. Each customer gets 5GB for free. Prime members enjoy free unlimited photo storage. To turn on the automatic back up option, do the following:

1. Go to **Photos** app and tap to expand the menu using the three horizontal lines in the top left.
2. Select **Settings**. You will see options to turn on Auto-save for photos and videos.
3. Select the files you want to back up.

Note it is advisable to start the backup process while your device is charging. When back up is successful, you can view them by visiting Amazon Drive Cloud and signing in with your Amazon account.

Turn off lock screen ads

The Kindle Fore tablet is affordable but you may have to battle with the ads enabled on the lock screen. The ads are for other Amazon products and services. If you aren't interested in them, you can disable them at a cost of $15. If you are willing to bear the extra cost, simply log in to your Amazon account on another computer and follow the steps below:

1. Visit your Devices page
2. Find your tablet on the list and click the button next to it. You will see the device is subscribed to Special Offers and Ads – click the **Edit** link.
3. Click on the button to unsubscribe.

Note that whether you are a Prime member or not, you will be charged $15.

Enable blue shade

The Kindle Fire can filter the blue light that can keep you up at night. To turn it on, consider the following steps;

1. Swipe from the top of the screen down and tap the **Blue Shade** icon.
2. The screen will immediately change color. You can adjust the color if you want. All you need to is go to Settings> Display> Blue Shade. There you can alternate brightness and set a schedule for it to activate automatically.

Uninstall apps

If you are on the home screen, it is quite easy to uninstall any app. Simply hold on an app icon for three seconds to get the uninstall option to pop up in the top right. You can select multiple apps if you so wish and get rid of them all.

Alternatively, go to Settings >Apps & Games > manage All Applications. Tap on the app you want to get rid of, and then tap **Uninstall** in the top right.

Share books like oxygen

As you get immersed in your book, you find that the feeling you get from what you're reading is just too wonderful to keep to yourself. You want to share to your family members so that others can see how excellent this author is. No hassle, you got the beloved **Kindle Family Library**

If you want to set this up,
1. Go to **Manage Your Content and services** on your Amson account
2. Move to the **settings** tab
3. Choose **Households and Family Library**
4. Select Invite Adult
5. Choose the buddy you want to include

From here onward, your accounts are now linked so you can share easily.

Make the battery last for ages

Okay you know it's not literal ages. But there's a way that you can make your Kindle's battery last longer – by using the Airplane mode. If you're not going to the kindle store or any internet thingy, just turn Airplane mode on

The kindle's battery already lasts super long. But you do this technique and your mind will be at rest regarding battery matters. When you turn on Airplane mode, it doesn't do any harm to your reading. You read and airplane mode is on – everyone is happy.

Take that Screenshot

And you thought you couldn't take screenshots. See it's not just your PC and phones that can take screenshots; even your Kindle has that superpower. If you're using the Kindle Paperwhite or Kindle Voyage, you long-pressing the two opposite corners of the screen at the same time.

With the Kindle touch, you can just Press and hold the Home button and Tap the display. If you use the original Kindle, Press the Alt+Shift+G. If you want to know that you got it right, the screen should flash. Your screen shots are all kept as .png files. And you can transfer it to your computer using a USB

Convert to Kindle

When you send other formats to you Kindle to read, it might not go as easy as you would imagine. The texts might how up too big or too small. The only way through is to transform it to the kindle format. And you can easily transform using your Send-to-Kindle email address.

To see you Send-to-Kindle email address,
1. Go to **Manage your contents and devices**
2. Then **Settings**
3. Move to **Personal Document settings**
4. Look under the **Send-to-Kindle email settings** for your email address.

Then to send to your device, just attach the document and address it to your Send -to-Kindle email address. In the subject line, add "convert".

Set security

No one likes prying eyes on their stuff. So If you want no one to go through you contents, you can just easily set a passcode.

1. Enter **Settings**
2. Then **Device Options**
3. Choose **Device passcode.**

From here you can set that passcode, just don't set something easily guessable.

Conclusion

I believe you enjoyed reading this guide. Well, it'll be great to have a recap on all we have said so far.

First, your Kindle Fire device is an impressive device. It was brilliantly created for the purpose of reading, though you can still execute other actions with it. And with the device, reading a book is just as easy as clicking on it and purchasing.

We also mentioned that you can easily delete a book with a long press and select **Remove device**. That method does not clear up your purchase records.

To clear that, you will need to go over to the **Manage your Content and Devices** section in your account, move to **Your Content**, select the book and delete.

Or you can easily deregister your account by choosing **Your Devices** in the **Manage your Content and Devices** and deregister.

When you're device starts acting up, the first thing you want to do is to restart it. If that doesn't work, then you can follow the steps outlined in this guide.

Steps like cleaning the screen when keyboard does not type well, pushing your cable further in when device does not charge and restarting network when it won't connect to Wi-Fi.

What about keeping notifications silent? We mentioned how to do this. Hit **Settings** then **Sounds and Notification**. You can also turn on **Blue shade** during the hours of the night by swiping down and turning it on. Or you want to change your wallpaper, just go to **Settings**, **Display** then **Wallpaper**.

Disclaimer

In as much as the author believes beginners will find this book helpful in learning how to use a Kindle Fire 8 and 10 devices, it is only a small book. It should not be relied upon solely for all Kindle Fire 8 and 10 tricks and troubleshooting.

About the author

Stephen Rock has been a certified apps developer and tech researcher for more than 12 years. Some of his 'how to' guides have appeared in a handful of international journals and tech blogs. He loves rabbits.

Facebook page @ Newcomers Guide

Also by the Author

1. IPHONE USER MANUAL FOR NEWCOMERS: All in one iOS 12 guide for beginners and seniors (iPhone, 8, X, XS & XS Max user guide)\
2. APPLE WATCH USER GUIDE FOR NEWCOMERS: The unofficial Apple Watch series 4 user manual for beginners and seniors
3. 3D PRINTING GUIDE FOR NEWCOMERS
4. SAMSUNG GALAXY S9 PLUS USER MANUAL FOR NEWCOMERS
5. IPAD INSTRUCTION GUIDE FOR NEWCOMERS
6. WINDOWS 10 USER MANUAL FOR NEWCOMERS

NOTES:

NOTES:

www.ingramcontent.com/pod-product-compliance
Lightning Source LLC
Chambersburg PA
CBHW031247050326

40690CB00007B/996